Cleve's Quotes

JUST THINGS TO PONDER

BARBARA J. WALKER

LifeRich
PUBLISHING®

LifeRich Publishing books may be ordered through booksellers or by contacting:

LifeRich Publishing
1663 Liberty Drive
Bloomington, IN 47403
www.liferichpublishing.com
844-686-9607

ISBN: 978-1-4897-4510-1 (sc)
ISBN: 978-1-4897-4509-5 (hc)
ISBN: 978-1-4897-4508-8 (e)

Library of Congress Control Number: 2020913154

Print information available on the last page.

LifeRich Publishing rev. date: 11/03/2022

Contents

Kingdom Principles

The only answer to all the rebellion and lawlessness is not writing brand-new laws. It is writing the law of the King on brand-new hearts.

There really will be a banquet in God's kingdom but with no hangovers, no dirty dishes, and no unwelcome guests.

Even on earth, God's will is always done, but in His kingdom, His will is always done without opposition.

The One who lifts up nations is also the One who brings them down. No human conspiracy can ever change that.

As God's kingdom ambassador, you must invite all people to enter the kingdom, but only the King can lead them in.

The good news of the kingdom is very bad news for those who steadfastly refuse to submit to the King.

Those longing for a utopia where everyone gets to choose their own "morality" will never see God's kingdom, unless they repent before it's too late.

The ruler of God's kingdom is the Prince of Peace, but He has a vast army that He will one day victoriously lead into battle.

Citizens of God's kingdom come from every family, tribe, culture, ethnicity, and nation, but they all come from only one race.

Citizenship in God's kingdom is only by the King's invitation. It's surrounded by a high and impenetrable wall.

Respect the authority of earthly kingdoms, unless their authority conflicts with the authority of God's kingdom.

God's kingdom is first and foremost a kingdom of love, but it is first and foremost a love for Him above all else.

God's plan is to one day bring every other kingdom under submission to His kingdom, except for the devil's kingdom. That kingdom He will destroy.

When you place yourself last on your list of priorities, God will place you first on His.

When someone asks you for your help, God will always provide you with something to give them—something even better than money, food, or clothing.

When God supplies your needs, He always provides a little extra so you can help provide for someone else's needs.

Child of God, Jesus doesn't call you to live a holy life to become holy. He calls you to live a holy life because you *are* holy.

Unlike today's culture, no one will be able to blame anyone else (not even the devil) for their failures when they stand before God.

People may choose those they will appoint, but only God can choose those He will anoint.

The Father's will is to glorify His Son. The Son's will is to glorify the Father. The Spirit's will is to reveal God's will.

Little Known Facts

Little known facts: Jesus said His bride would be known by her love for Him and for each other, not for a love based on skin color.

Little known facts: Jesus talked more about a literal place of eternal torment than anybody else in the Bible.

Little known facts: Jesus said Israel was the only nation that worshipped the true God, but they refused to honor the One the true God sent.

Little known facts: Jesus said those who obey Him are the true children of Abraham and those who don't are the devil's children.

Little known facts: Jesus said the next time Israel saw Him they'd say, "Blessed is He who comes in the Name of the Lord" (Matthew 23:39 NIV).

Little known facts: Jesus said we should read the Old Testament prophet Daniel to better understand what will take place during the end times.

Little known facts: Jesus spoke about Adam and Eve as real people and used them to explain God's ordained design for marriage.

Little known facts: Jesus believed the flood of Noah actually happened and used it to describe how taken by surprise folks will be about the next big prophetic event.

Little known facts: Although they rejected and crucified Him, Jesus did not permanently reject Israel. He is still rightly called the Son of David.

Little known facts: Jesus believed that the entire Old Testament testified about Him and that no one can fully appreciate Him if they don't read it.

Little known facts: While here, Jesus never did a single thing in His own power and authority. He depended completely on His Father, as He wants us to do.

Little known facts: Jesus was the humblest man on earth, but throughout His entire ministry and even during His darkest hours, He never backed down from a confrontation with evil.

Little known facts: Jesus did indeed invite sinners to come to Him just as they are, but He never desired sinners to stay as they are and always told them so.

Little known facts: Jesus never said or did anything to win the approval of people or to keep them as His followers.

Little known facts: Jesus left no room for a middle ground. If you're not for Him, you're against Him. (Sorry, moderates.)

Little known facts: Jesus demonstrated more than once that only God controls the wind, rain, and sea. (Sorry, climate changers.)

Little known facts: Jesus never condemned or justified anyone based on skin color. To Him, all hearts matter. (Sorry, BLM.)

Little known facts: Jesus meant it when He said, "Pray for your enemies." (Sorry, flesh.)

Little known facts: Jesus wants you to live in expectancy of His soon return, but He also wants you to be prepared for the long haul.

Little known facts: Jesus is the Prince of Peace, but He carries a sword that divides those who love Him from those who don't.

Little known facts: Jesus is the Prince of Peace, but it's a peace between God and man. There can be no peace for the wicked.

Little known facts: Jesus is the Prince of Peace, but He has fought many battles and decisively won every single one.

Little known facts: Jesus does indeed have a burden He wants you to bear, but His burden won't weigh you down or wear you out.

Little known facts: You cannot possibly love your loved ones more than Jesus loves them.

Little known facts: Jesus wants you to love Him even more than you love your loved ones.

Little known facts: Jesus didn't send the Comforter to only comfort you. He sent Him so you might be able to comfort others.

Little known facts: Jesus is not more patient or kinder than the God of the Old Testament. They are One in mercy and in wrath.

Little known facts: Even Jesus doesn't yet know the day or the hour of His return.

Little known facts: Jesus actually found great joy and delight in obeying the Ten Commandments.

Little known facts: Jesus didn't seek a large number of fans. He even discouraged such people from following Him.

Little known facts: There were times when Jesus sighed, cried, groaned, mourned, shouted, and laughed.

Little known facts: Just like the rest of us, even Jesus had a hard time saying no to His mother.

Little known facts: Jesus really does love the little children: red and yellow, black and white, and those still in the womb.

Little known facts: Jesus didn't come to free us to do what we want to do. He came to free us to do what we ought to do.

Little known facts: Jesus is the most hated man in history, and He promised that those who follow Him will also be hated.

Little known facts: Jesus has met the founding prophets of all major religions, but He's not the one doing the bowing.

Little known facts: Jesus did not come to judge or condemn anyone, but He promised that one day He would do both.

Little known facts: Jesus defined what God's design for marriage, gender, and family is.

Little known facts: Jesus spoke a great deal about evil—the evil in every person, the evil in the world, and the evil one.

Little known facts: One of the people whose faith impressed Jesus the most was a military leader who owned slaves.

Little known facts: Jesus never gave suggestions about how people should live. He gave commandments.

Little known facts: While Jesus was here, He didn't do any works He doesn't expect His followers to do, except rising from the dead in our own power.

A Paradox

A paradox: With God it is your inability that qualifies you to be mightily used by Him.

A paradox: The sooner we realize that God's ways are not our ways, the sooner our ways will conform to His ways.

A paradox: There is no end to God's mercy, but although it is long, there is an end to His patience.

A paradox: The same God who blesses the things that please Him also curses the things that displease Him.

A paradox: God deals with individuals based on their choices, but He deals with nations based on the choices of their leaders.

A paradox: Parents shouldn't treat their kids as if they belong to them. They should treat them as if they belong to God.

A paradox: There's no difference between those who deny God's existence and those who acknowledge Him but live like He doesn't exist.

A paradox: It is possible to be angry and not sin, but it is impossible to rage without sinning.

A paradox: True love is always best displayed when you show love to those who do not return your love.

A paradox: Jesus sets people free not to do what they want to do but what they ought to do.

A paradox: God is everywhere at all times, but His Presence is not *with* everyone on earth.

A paradox: When society rejects the restrictions of God's laws, it will create myriad laws that are much more restrictive.

A paradox: A world desperately seeking to create a utopia will want no part of a paradise that requires holiness.

A paradox: Whenever darkness and evil abound, God's amazing grace abounds so much more.

A paradox: You can be a child of God all by yourself, but you cannot mature in your faith apart from other children of God.

A paradox: God permits many nations to successfully attack Israel because of its rebellion, but great will be the judgment of those nations that do.

A paradox: A child of God should endeavor to be friendly, but they should not try to be everybody's friend.

A paradox: Any friend who expects you to do everything they ask is not a real friend, unless that friend is Jesus.

A paradox: Traditional matrimony is between a man and a woman. Holy matrimony is between a man, a woman, and God.

A paradox: This world is even worse off than it appears, but Jesus Christ is much more glorious than you can possibly imagine.

Things the Church Forgot

Things the church forgot: His church doesn't call for world unity. It calls people out of the world and into unity with Jesus.

Things the church forgot: Jesus is coming back for a church that has overcome the world despite its suffering, just as He did.

Things the church forgot: It is better not to preach at all than to preach half truth, because a half truth is a whole lie.

Things the church forgot: God Himself ordained government just as He ordained marriage, and He blesses both only if they honor Him.

Things the church forgot: Living a life that pleases God is a life that is not trying to please the world or yourself.

Things the church forgot: The blood of Jesus is the remedy for sin, not an excuse for it.

You can either live to please God or you can live to please the world, but you cannot do both. Anyone who tells you different is from the evil one.

A good reputation with friends, family, and the general public is a good thing to have. A good reputation with God is the *best* thing to have. (June 13, 2012)

Maybe I'm crazy or just plain naïve, but I have a vision of America, one day, celebrating the birth of Christ without apologies to skeptics or undue deference to world religions. Merry Christmas, everyone. (December 15, 2011)

Contrary to popular opinion, God has not changed His mind on sin. Every single transgression of His law will be paid for, one way or another.

Father, we have forgotten our mission. We cry out for escape and deliverance from the very battles You have called us to fight.

As we acknowledge the award of the Masters coveted green jacket, let us rejoice that *the* Master adorns His victorious ones in the bright linen robe of righteousness.

Jesus Christ did not come to accommodate, reform, or fix the works of the devil. He came to destroy them.

Because Jesus overcame the world, so too shall His church prevail, but as it was with Jesus, the world will think it has won—for a little while.

What's God's response to any who cannot understand His Triune nature? "I AM WHO I AM."

Bible

If we read the whole Bible, we'd know why the devil desperately tries to keep us from reading the whole Bible.

If we read the Bible, we'd know the only One who can change the climate is the One who changes everything else.

Hmmm. Why are so many people who claim to know the end of the book reacting like those who never read any page of it?

If we paid more heed to the divine mandates in the Bible than we do to human mandates, we wouldn't be in this mess.

The most amazing thing is that so many are surprised that what the Bible said would happen is actually happening.

These are the times we'll see who actually believes the Bible or who cherry-picks it for parts that don't demand obedience.

If you're more worked up about what the evil one is doing than what the Holy One is doing, you don't really believe the Bible.

As experts agonize over motives for increased destructive and self-destructive behavior, perhaps it's time to reread what the Bible says about the devil.

If you want your life to be fruitful for God, you must study the Bible. There can be no good fruit if Good Seed is not planted.

Ironically, there are numerous atheists in this world, but there is not a single atheist in hell.

Without the Bible

Contrary to popular opinion, we cannot fully appreciate the whole counsel of God without studying the entire Bible—both the Old Testament and the New Testament.

Without Isaiah, Jeremiah, and the other prophets, we wouldn't know that God always sends warnings to His people before He brings judgment.

Without the Song of Songs, we wouldn't know how intimate and passionate the divine romance is between God and His people.

Without Ecclesiastes, we wouldn't know the vanity and vexation of trying to live a truly fulfilling life apart from God.

Without Proverbs, we wouldn't understand that the wisdom of God and the wisdom of man have absolutely nothing to do with each other.

Without Psalms, we wouldn't know about the Shepherd who safely leads His sheep through the darkest valleys to the still waters of peace.

Without Job, we wouldn't know that the sign of God's approval on a person's life is not outward prosperity. It is the inward fruit produced by a steadfast heart.

Without Esther, we wouldn't know that God can use one person in the right place at the right time to save an entire nation.

Without Chronicles, Ezra, and Nehemiah, we wouldn't see how God still continues to bless His own, even in the midst of His judgment.

Without 1 and 2 Kings, we wouldn't know that good and evil leaders are a blessing or a judgment from the Lord.

Without 1 and 2 Samuel, we wouldn't see that people judge others by outward appearance, but God looks into the hearts of the humble to find kings.

Without Ruth, we wouldn't see how God can bring great love and redemption out of great misfortune and loss.

Without Judges, we wouldn't see that confusion, discord, and violence always come when everyone does what is right in their own eyes.

Without Joshua, we wouldn't know God raises up nations and brings them down according to His own purposes.

Without Leviticus, Numbers, and Deuteronomy, we wouldn't understand that only God gets to declare what is clean and unclean—holy and unholy.

Without Exodus, we'd never know that when God declares a nation's boundaries, it would be wise for other nations not to challenge His decree.

Without Genesis, we'd never know about the time when sinful people actually broke the heart of their Creator.

Attributes

Rest doesn't come from ceasing all your labors. It comes from ceasing all labors that bear no fruit in God.

Faith isn't preparation for dealing with the future. It is strength and power to act in the present.

Progress doesn't mean just forging straight ahead. It means going in the right direction even if that means going back the way you came.

Compassion is not a warm, fuzzy feeling that comes from helping grateful people. It is helping people despite their ungratefulness.

Prosperity is not possessing anything your heart wants. It is not letting anything that you have possess your heart.

Security doesn't come from hiding from danger. It comes from seeking it and defeating it.

Reconciliation doesn't come from airing grievances. It comes from forgiving them.

Anger and rage are not the same. Anger moved David to slay a wicked giant. Rage moved a mob to crucify an innocent man. So before you blow up, grow up.

God is an investor. He gave you this day while expecting you to give it back to Him with interest, namely 100 percent increase in your love for Him.

He spoke, and a billion galaxies burst into existence. He will speak again, and all creation will be renewed. Amid all voices today, it is His voice we must respond to.

With the evidence of the handiwork of a Creator all around us, a person has to have *waaaay* too much blind faith to remain an atheist. (August 17, 2012)

Father, we have become foolish servants. We have exchanged Your wisdom for worldly philosophies of success, tolerance, and human potential.

No matter what happens or doesn't happen today, Christ followers are the only people who always have reason for hope.

Child of God, if you let this world's hatred provoke you to hate, you have been overcome by the world.

Attitude Checks

Attitude check: Followers of Jesus shouldn't live in dread of what the devil and his followers are doing. We should live in continual awe of what God has done.

Attitude check: It is great presumption to say "never" about something unless it is about something God has said "never" to.

Attitude check: Do you feel disgust with those flaunting their perversions but no pity for souls being publicly devoured?

Attitude check: Are you more anguished about the attempts to steal our freedoms than the attempts to steal God's glory?

Attitude check: If God showed you mercy when you opposed Him, are you praying for Him to show mercy to those who oppose you?

Attitude check: The rod of God's discipline will definitely hurt, but it is always wielded in love.

Attitude check: While we bemoan the actions of a wicked multitude, all of heaven throws a party when even one sinner repents.

God is not looking for a strong person to serve Him. He's looking for a weak person who will choose to walk in His strength.

Despite the weather or the headlines, any day God gives you is another opportunity to honor Him, which makes it a truly glorious day.

God has a plan for you today that includes blessing you and you being a blessing. You would be wise to humbly submit all your plans to His plan.

Sin is exceedingly sinful not just because of its terrible impact on us but because it is, first and foremost, an offense against a Holy God.

Child of God, don't fear God because you're afraid He'll stop loving you. Reverently fear Him because He firmly disciplines those He loves.

Today, Jesus will give you the chance to serve people like He did. How and if you do it will determine if you are religious or redeemed.

Will you gladly follow Jesus anywhere He leads, or will you ask Him to follow you to where you want to go?

So are you excited about living for Jesus during these climactic times? Or are you just closing your eyes and hoping it all just goes away.

God never intended for all people to have the exact same possessions and talents. He intended for all people to use 100 percent of whatever they had for His glory.

Pity is a precious ointment when you apply it to the wounded heart of another, but it becomes a slow killing poison when you apply it to yourself.

It's OK if you lose your mind today, as long as God is the One who finds it.

A real friend might hurt you with the truth, while a false friend will comfort you with a lie.

As we come to the end of another week and anticipate a weekend break, remember that God is the kind of Father who wants full custody of His kids, not just weekend visitations.

Until we understand the exceeding awfulness of sin, we will never fully appreciate the only One who can save from sin.

The worst sins are unrepented sins and the worst sinners are unrepentant sinners who influence other sinners to be unrepentant.

People call seeking common ground between the holy and the unholy loving compromise. God calls it an abomination.

People call prioritizing anything or anyone—including yourself—ahead of serving God just being practical. God calls it idolatry.

People call regularly praying and worshipping God while disobeying His commandments "religion." God calls it using His name in vain.

People call giving a person's earnings to others who didn't earn it "reparations." God calls it stealing.

People call abortion a woman's right to choose. God still calls it murder.

Child of God, as sure as the sun rises and sets, you will experience loss. Joy comes from focusing on what you will never lose.

You will always completely misunderstand God's ways if you think His ways can ever be completely understood.

The moment you think you have God's ways all figured out is the moment you ceased to grow in your faith.

Gratitude

Father, we thank You for all the medical breakthroughs that You have inspired, but forgive us for placing all our hope in them.

It's amazing how much blessed assurance will flood your soul when you finally come to understand that *everything* belongs to God.

If you can't believe the Creator spoke an entire universe into existence to share it with a small remnant on one planet, you just cannot grasp the generosity of God.

Being who you are is no great accomplishment, but being who God created you to be is cause for great rejoicing.

Child of God, we do not serve Jesus to be forgiven. We serve Him because we *are* forgiven. It's the difference between love and fear.

I am thankful for the gift of true friends. I could never be all God wants me to be without them, and neither can you.

You cannot give God anything He does not already own. You can only surrender to Him your claim to it.

You'll know that you have learned the secret of contentment when you can joyfully say, "Thank God it's Monday!"

There has never been anything in this world as beautiful as what awaits us in heaven, except the only One who came down from heaven.

Earthly Fathers

If I have learned anything about being a husband, it came from a dad who treated my momma like she was a gift from God.

Like everyone, my dad had his flaws. He wasn't a perfect father, but his life made it much easier for me to place all my trust in a Father who is.

Daddy had a fierce love. If my brothers and I had joined a gang, it wouldn't be the police we'd be worried about.

I was born in the segregated South, but my daddy taught us to see everyone as people created in the image of God—and accountable to Him first for their actions.

My dad had little formal education, but teachers, community leaders, pastors, and neighbors turned to him when they really needed wise counsel.

When I think of manhood, my first thought is always of my dad, the one who showed me that to be truly masculine is to be a man of God.

Love

No genuine act of love is ever a waste, even if that is act is completely unappreciated by those who benefit from it.

Whatever you most fear in this life will eventually make you betray what you most love.

God's preferred method of teaching a person how to love is placing at least one extremely difficult person in their life.

Child of God, if you cannot humbly receive the discipline of your Heavenly Father, you cannot experience His love.

God doesn't need your love, but you desperately need to love Him. It's what you were created to do and anything else you do is worthless if you don't.

Good news! God loves you just as you are! Better news! He loves you too much to leave you that way.

Agape: a love that loves you and loves those you love more than you ever could and moves you to love those who don't love you.

God didn't command us to like people. He commanded us to love them. There is a big difference.

You will see God do many more miracles when you understand His greatest miracle is His presence in the heart of those who love Him.

Love Grown Cold

In the eyes of Jesus, your love has grown cold if you only love those who love you.

Your love has grown cold if you don't care what the devil does, as long as he leaves you and yours alone.

Your love has grown cold if you are satisfied with worshipping Jesus only once a week.

Your love has grown cold when you treat others based on the way they treat you.

Your love has grown cold when fear of rejection makes you quench the Holy Spirit by keeping your faith to yourself.

Your love has grown cold if you have written someone off as a lost cause.

Your love has grown cold if you can reach out to unbelievers but feel nothing but disdain for church people who are deceived by Satan.

Your love has grown cold when forgiving others is something you never ask God to do when you pray.

Your love has grown cold if the safety and well-being of you and yours are all that matters to you.

Your love has grown cold if you take pleasure in thinking about your enemies facing the wrath of Almighty God.

The big question that should be asked is not "Why has the world grown so hateful?" It is "Has your love grown cold?"

Father, our love has grown cold. We mock and curse the unbelievers You died for and bite and devour our own wounded brethren.

Legalism is the worship of laws. Grace is worshiping the only One who fulfilled God's law to put His law on our hearts.

He Cares

Child of God, you may feel like an orphaned child, but you have a Father who calls you His family and a Brother who sacrificed everything for you.

You will feel lonely, but you are never alone. You will feel rejected, but you are always welcomed. You will feel unworthy, but you are always highly favored.

If you believe everything you have belongs to God—including yourself—what can the enemy steal from you?

The One who will return to receive His own longs for that day so much more than our own yearning to see His return.

Child of God, the One who never changes promises you that everything else will change. The world will change from bad to worse, but you will be changed from glory to glory.

When you give all your cares to God, the only cares that you will ever have are for those who have *not* given them to Him.

Child of God, He still has much He wants you to do and to be in this life, but His main purpose has always been to prepare you for eternity.

Prayer

Contrary to popular theory, *the* reason this nation survived and thrived is because Americans of all skin colors prayed.

Contrary to popular opinion, it's good to pray for patience. If you don't pray for it, then God will teach you to pray for it.

Facebook friend: "Cleve, why do we even need to pray if God already knows what we need?" Me: "Because He commands us to."

There is no weapon—no matter how massive—in this world that can rival the power that is released by a single childlike prayer.

Some of the most powerfully effective prayers are the ones we pray when it feels like we don't have any more prayers left to pray.

The devil mocks at our impotent rage against him, but he greatly trembles before our earnest prayers.

Much knowledge comes from much study, but genuine wisdom only comes from asking God for it in prayer.

Every victory in your life was preceded by prayer, by you or by someone praying for you.

Earnestly praying for people is God's preferred method for making radical change in their lives and in yours.

Praying throughout the day is the difference between fighting battles on your own and God fighting them on your behalf.

Beginning each day with prayer is the difference between feeling helpless and knowing there is nothing that God can't do.

God's yeses and noes to our prayers are directly related to our yeses and noes to His commands.

Father, we have turned away from You. We have minimized sin because we are ashamed of the bloody cross carried by Your Son.

The most powerful weapon on earth is prayer, and like any weapon, you must be wise in how you handle it and where you aim it.

Praying for people we love is a very natural prayer, but praying forgiveness and blessings on those who hate us is the Lord's prayer.

When we pray for God to change people, we really mean to make them someone we could like, but that's never why God changes people.

A morning prayer: while this world rants and rages against the holiness of God, may His praise ever be on our lips.

Don't waste time praying that this world would stop being so dark. Pray that God would let Jesus's light shine brighter in you.

As we call on God today, remember nothing can rob the effectiveness of prayer like a heart filled with unforgiveness.

Peace

You will only have God's peace in your home when God's peace has a home in your heart.

Real peace for Jesus followers doesn't come from the absence of battles. It comes from knowing all our battles belong to God.

World peace cannot happen because the world loves only itself. Genuine peace comes only from loving the Prince of Peace above all else.

Real and lasting peace between people doesn't come from just agreeing to disagree. It only comes when people completely agree with God.

For the child of God, living in His peace doesn't come from avoiding all the chaos. It comes from overcoming it.

The peace that Jesus offers is not a gift you have to frantically hold onto. It is a gift that holds onto you.

The peace that surpasses all understanding cannot be experienced by those who lean on their own understanding.

Just like all of God's gifts, nothing and no one can steal the peace He gives you, but you can choose to surrender it to them.

We will not see peace in America until we first make peace with God, and that will not happen until His people turn back to Him.

The peace that Jesus offers does not depend on peaceful surroundings. It is the supernatural overflow from a Spirit-filled heart.

Peace is not the absence of conflict. It is the presence of the Holy Spirit in the midst of conflict.

So lasting is the peace that Jesus gives that no power on earth can ever take it away from you, but you can give it away. Don't.

Calling

God's calling on your life will always require great patience as He prepares you to carry it out.

God's calling on your life will always place you in direct opposition to the way the world does things.

God's calling on your life will always be infused with a burning desire to serve Him and to serve others.

God's calling on your life will always involve doing something that seems beyond your abilities to do.

A good friend will recognize your calling in life. Your best friend will help you fulfill that calling.

Because a religious bigot answered a calling to greatly suffer for the One he once zealously persecuted, he is forever enshrined as God's trophy of grace.

Because a humble young woman said yes to an impossible calling, she proved for all time that all things are possible with God.

Because a strangely garbed vagabond in the wilderness answered God's calling, he got to introduce the bride of Christ to the Bridegroom.

Because a poor widow answered the calling to give all that she had, she became an eternal symbol of what it means to be rich in God's eyes.

Because Abraham answered God's calling to leave the security of home to wander through perilous lands, he became the father of nations and of all who have faith.

Because David tended and sang over a small flock of sheep, God called him to be the psalmist/king over an entire nation.

Some of the biggest events in history happened because someone was faithful to fulfill what seemed like only a very small calling.

Some of the tears the Bible says God will wipe away may include tears of regret for not fulfilling His calling in our lives.

The American church has a calling, and it is not to just be silent as heathens parade their immorality before innocent children.

The first Adam ran and hid from God's calling. The last Adam gladly embraced His Father's calling. How have you responded to your calling?

You are still alive because God still has a calling on your life. His retirement plan for you begins after you leave this life.

If you really want to be sure you are walking in your calling, walk closer to the One who gave you the calling.

Don't get them confused. Your job is what you do. Your calling is what you are.

The greatest calling that God places on a person's life is a calling that helps other people fulfill His calling for their lives.

Your job is work you do while expecting to be paid for it. Your calling is work you'd do even if you had to pay for the chance to do it.

Every day God gives you is another day He uses to prepare you for eternity and to help you prepare others for eternity.

Child of God, the Father sent the Son. The Son sent the Holy Spirit. The Holy Spirit sends you.

Job of the Believer

Facebook friend: Cleve, why should we keep trying to tell people what they refuse to hear, and why should we keep trying to change things that will not change? Me: God does not hold us responsible for those who will not listen, and He does not demand we succeed in changing a world that is doomed to fail. All God commands is that His people speak the truth and do whatever is in our power to do. (August 23, 2013)

With the news of young people maiming and murdering just for the fun of it, the answer is *not* more psychological help or more gun laws. We are overrun with the names of psychotic disorders and inundated with a multitude of brand-name laws and ordinances. The answer is the same as ever: turn to the only One who can renew minds and write His laws on the heart. (August 22, 2013)

When a good person remains silent in the face of evil, they give their consent to that evil. (August 21, 2013)

If you are vexed about all the things the wicked are doing, the most important question to ask God is "What do You want the righteous to be doing?"

Your Words

What would you do if you found out that what troubles your heart is not the words of others but the words from your own mouth?

If you really bit your tongue before you spoke evil about someone, you might end up with a swollen tongue, but you'd also have a lighter heart.

If you knew every single word you speak echoes into eternity, would you choose your words more carefully?

It's impolite to speak while someone else is talking to you, but it's far worse to speak while God is talking to you.

Flattering words feel good but don't do a person any good. Truthful but encouraging words make a person feel better and do better.

When the devil gets a person to speak the words he speaks, then his lies become their reality.

Speaking the truth without love is sinful, but so is not speaking the truth to avoid being rejected.

A lie can be soothing in the beginning but, if believed, ends in great pain. The truth may hurt at the start but, if received, brings much healing.

Respectful discourse should always be the goal, but it is better to hear rudely spoken truths than to listen to eloquently spoken lies.

Testing

Season of testing will come, but during such times, remember no one has ever bent as low or has been raised as high as Jesus.

What seems like one painful loss after another may be the Master Gardener pruning a fruitful life to produce even more fruit.

To hear what a person believes, listen to them. To see what a person believes, watch them. To know what a person believes, behold them in their suffering.

Is Jesus worth the rejection by friends and family, or do you adjust your faith to make your relationship work?

Will you gladly stand with Jesus and be thought a fool or seek to placate those who are very wise in their own eyes?

True wisdom comes from understanding that our greatest joys and darkest tragedies are not the ones that happen in this life.

Father, we are spoiled children. Help us to humbly accept Your rod of discipline and to remember that You only chasten those You love. Amen.

Jesus was the only person who could truthfully say He never did or said anything to deserve His sufferings.

You will look like a fool to either people or to God. It's the difference between temporary rejection and eternal rejection.

As the darkness began to enshroud His soul, even Jesus wanted His friends to be near Him. Don't walk through dark times without your friends.

When you're feeling lonely, remember no one has ever felt as isolated as Jesus felt or been asked to do what He was asked.

Jesus didn't suffer and die to spare you from suffering and death in this life. He did it so your earthly suffering would never be in vain.

God is always more focused on what you let Him do in your own heart than what you are asking Him to do in someone else.

If you're comfortable with everything God's doing in your life, take a second look, because most of what He does will rub you the wrong way.

Be patient child of God. It is impossible for the One who began time and who will end time to ever be too late.

You will offend some people no matter how you try to avoid it. So relax and just avoid offending God. What He approves or condemns is all that really matters.

Warfare

Fellow warriors, please understand this: Surrender to anything but God won't help you escape spiritual war. It just makes you a casualty.

God has plans for you. The devil also has plans for you, but his plans for you can only work when you resist God's plans.

Don't focus on the shifting conspiracies of the wicked. Fix your attention on the unshakable plans of God, and He will establish you in His peace.

You will have fewer enemies in this world if you just compromise and go along with the flow, but the One enemy you *will* have is a real doozy.

A lot of folk picture Jesus as a docile, harmless teacher. They do not realize that when Jesus came to earth the first time, it was as God's Sacrificial Lamb. One day He will return to deal with those who refused His sacrifice. (August 1, 2013)

Believer, if you really understood the vast power God has arrayed around you and placed within you, it'd be much easier for you to pity your enemies.

Child of God, your struggle is with the unseen evil behind the evil we see—an evil that only fears weapons that are also unseen.

I Wonder

I used to wonder how long it would take schools to decay after they outlawed public prayer. I don't wonder about that anymore.

I used to wonder if American churches would become secular and compromising like European churches. I don't wonder about that anymore.

I used to wonder if America would ever declare its independence from God. I no longer wonder about that.

I used to wonder how the devil could deceive entire nations like the Bible said he would. I don't wonder about that anymore.

Strange but True

Strange but true: Even great evil doesn't seem to be really all that evil, until it impacts you.

Strange but true: The more you think you understand about God, the more you will misunderstand Him.

Strange but true: Many people are desperately praying for God to deliver them out of situations that He chose to put them in.

Strange but true: It's hard to pray for someone you dislike, but it becomes harder to dislike someone you continually pray for.

Strange but true: You are always a big part of God's answer to your prayer for others.

Strange but true: Worry is not a lack of faith. It is just having more faith in your problems than in your God.

Strange but true: The best way to cultivate really healthy relationships is to ask God to pick your friends.

Strange but true: When you continually remain silent about the truth, you have become a habitual liar.

Strange but true: If you really believe what the Bible says, even all the bad news is part of the good news.

Strange but true: A lot of folks get no answer to their prayers because they pray like they're giving God advice.

Strange but true: The worst thing you can do to someone who is wasteful with money is to give them money.

Strange but true: The people who are demanding friendship are some of the unfriendliest people you'll ever meet.

Strange but true: Many who want nothing to do with God or His people will actually end up getting exactly what they want.

Strange but true: Our current government is completely hostile to Christianity because it wants to be America's only savior.

Strange but true: The thing that bugs you the most about someone else is the very same thing God is dealing with in you.

UFOs

Personally, even though it was a cute movie, I always thought ET looked a little demonic, but that's just me.

The Bible says "the prince of the power of the air" can appear as a being of light. So a bright spinning orb in the sky is no problem for Him.

All the speculation about UFOs is distracting folks from what God is really doing on the earth. That alone should tell us what they really are.

The Creator has created a dark dimension to consign all evil celestial beings, the one who leads them, and the people who followed them forever.

The benevolent celestial beings who visit our planet have been depicted as chubby little cherubs. That doesn't describe the two who destroyed Sodom and Gomorrah.

Jesus Himself met some of the evil celestial beings who stalk our planet. They were no more eager to encounter Him then than they are now.

The Bible shows how to tell which nations are overseen by evil celestial beings. They are the nations that persecute Jews and Christians.

The Bible says a celestial being is assigned to watch over the nation of Israel. His name is Michael, and he will stand up for Israel during its darkest hours.

Despite the silence of the American church on the subject, the Bible says there are celestial beings among us. Some of them are evil, and some of them actually oversee nations.

Earth has always been visited by powerful beings from another dimension. Some are sent on missions of benevolence, and others on missions of malevolence.

The Bible even speaks about highly intelligent alien body snatchers who hastily left their victims whenever Jesus showed up.

The Bible speaks about a star wars rebellion. A third of the warriors fell in defeat before the greatest force in the universe.

The Bible speaks about close encounters with beings not of this earth. One of them even convinced humankind that God could lie.

The Bible speaks about glowing lights that defy the laws of physics. Jesus Himself saw one fall “like lightning from Heaven.”

The Times

Uh, preachers, this weather and this generation make it a perfect time to preach on the most unpopular topic in the Bible.

These are the days we will easily see who lives in dread and who lives in hope-filled anticipation.

These are the times we will see just how far we will go to avoid being rejected by people, especially by friends and family.

These are the times we will see if the love that believers profess for others is based solely on whether or not they love us.

These are the times when we will see if our faith is based on the things we can see or the things we cannot see.

These are the times when we will really see those who faithfully attend church but are actually ashamed of Jesus and His cross.

These are the times when we'll find out if the people we thought we really knew are people we really want to know.

In the end times, we'll see counterfeit signs, wonders, and miracles because God is still genuine signs, wonders, and miracles.

In the last days, there will be two characteristics that will greatly distinguish God's people from those who are not His people. The first will be a genuine, honest-to-goodness love and unfeigned affection between those who belong to Jesus. The second will be a deep and abiding peace of mind. (August 23, 2013)

Just so you're absolutely clear on where things stand in our nation, here is a summation: In today's American society, the worst thing you can do is offend someone, and the worst offense it to tell another adult that they are responsible for the consequences of their own choices. (August 22, 2013)

The best way to be prepared for the unknown is to know the One for whom nothing is unknown.

Media

Old Glory has always flown proudly over the "land of the free," and it has been lovingly draped over the coffins of its brave soldiers. Our flag has also been scorned and desecrated by those who hate what it represents. After surviving "bombs bursting in air," it now faces its greatest test ever, and only God knows if it may soon be flown at half-mast due to the death of liberty.

If you are concerned about all the unjust laws and evil executive orders coming from Washington in the New Year, here's what God has to say about the situation: "The Lord foils the plans of the nations; he thwarts the purposes of the peoples. But the plans of the Lord stand firm forever, the purposes of his heart through all generations" (Psalm 33:10). Happy New Year, everybody! (December 31, 2012)

If you want to know just how slimy and degraded our culture's idea of entertainment and fun has become, just watch an episode of *The Andy Griffith Show*. Good-bye, Andy. Thanks for the memories of a time when the family could watch TV and laugh together at something that was not shameful. (July 3, 2013)

I am so thankful that there are more hardworking, freedom-loving, God-fearing Americans than the media would have us believe. I am especially thankful that some of them are my friends.

Lesson from the Pandemic

Lessons from the pandemic: Science can never eradicate all disease because there is only One who has the power over sin's curse.

Lessons from the pandemic: A lot of folks who read the Bible were totally shocked to find out it is actually true.

Lessons from the pandemic: Beware any leadership—political or religious—that discourages courage but brandishes fear like a weapon.

Lessons from the pandemic: Some people genuinely deserve our respect and confidence, but no human being deserves our complete, unquestioning faith.

Lessons from the pandemic: For a healthier life, physically getting together with friends and family is as essential as eating.

Lessons from the pandemic: The difference between medical "miracles" and divine healing is one never has any negative side effects with the latter.

Lessons from the pandemic: When the church compromises the faith to change a fallen world, we don't change it. It changes us.

Wake Up, America

Our leaders have us at each other's throats, fomenting violence, envy, and division in the name of an idol called "equity." Wake up, America!

Israel battles for its very survival while its greatest ally—despite warning from God—seeks common cause with its worst enemies. Wake up, America!

Wicked leaders are fixated on the fantasy of climate change while law enforcement is hamstrung, leaving entire cities plagued with lawless violence. Wake up, America!

Even evil rulers in China, Russia, and Iran aren't pushing perversions like transgenderism on their kids! Wake up, America!

I believe God granted this power grab to teach America humility. So would you please hurry up and learn it before these folks completely destroy us?

It's really amazing that so many people are *so* surprised that after letting Darwin teach our children that humans are just like animals, so many choose to act like animals. (August 23, 2013)

Ultimately, there is no lasting hope for this world, but there is an eternal hope for those who desire to leave its darkness behind.

America is learning the hard way that changing the name of evil into something else doesn't make it any less evil.

CPSIA information can be obtained
at www.ICGtesting.com
Printed in the USA
LVHW041843261122
734045LV00003B/8

9 781489 745095